In this series –

RUMI READINGS
FOR
COLLEGE

RUMI READINGS
FOR
COLLEGE

JALALUDDIN RUMI

The Scheherazade Foundation

The Scheherazade Foundation CIC
85 Great Portland Street
London
W1W 7LT
United Kingdom
www.SF.Charity
info@SF.Charity

First published by The Scheherazade Foundation CIC, 2025

RUMI READINGS FOR COLLEGE

A CIP catalogue record for this title is available from the British Library.

ISBN 978-1-915311-70-2

Introduction

Jalaluddin Rumi was born in Balkh, Afghanistan, in the year 1207, and died in Konya, Turkey, in 1273.

During the sixty-six years spanning this pair of dates, he produced a range of extraordinary work in Persian which, today, is classed as 'Sufi Mysticism'.

In the seven and a half centuries since his death, Rumi's corpus, which includes *The Masnavi* and *Fihi Ma Fihi*, has been circulated widely across the Near East, the Arab world, and Central Asia.

Generations of students continue to commit selections of the 60,000 verses to heart, and allow Rumi's way of thought to permeate through all areas of their lives.

Although Orientalists venturing eastward from Europe in the 1700s occasionally made note of Sufi Mysticism, they tended to witness it through the more theatrical frills – such as 'whirling dervishes' – rather than through a deep appreciation of the texts.

It wasn't until the close of the nineteenth century that the first wholescale translations of Rumi's written work began to appear in Europe.

Even then, they remained very much the purview of a few academics, whose translations were – even for the time – laden with indescribably floral and cumbersome prose.

Although in the Occident, students would find themselves scrutinizing Rumi's corpus, it wasn't until more recently that accessible appreciations of his work became available.

A few years before his death, I asked my father – the Sufi scholar and thinker Idries Shah – for his thoughts on Rumi's legacy in the West.

Sitting in his favourite chair, a porcelain cup of green tea in hand, he looked at me hard.

'I never cease to be amazed,' he said.

'Amazed by what?'

'By the way people don't take what's perfectly packaged, and ready and waiting for them, but rather obsess with something else.'

'With what?'

'With endless and nonsensical trimmings, trappings, and paraphernalia.'

My father sipped his tea.

After a moment of silent thought, he continued:

'Read Rumi in the original Persian,' he said, 'and so delicate are the verses that you have tears rolling down your cheeks. Yet here in the West, it's served up as something submerged in a thick, glutinous gravy, so much so that its utterly inedible.'

I reminded my father that a series of publications had recently found their way to press – publications that presented Rumi's couplets in an utterly new way.

Stripped bare of what my father had referred to as 'gravy', they were light.

Indeed, they were lighter than light.

My father rolled his eyes at the thought.

'In any other place, and at any other time,' he said, 'people would be up in arms. Or, if they weren't, they'd be laughing until their sides split. Imagine it – Western poets with absolutely no knowledge of the original Persian text touting new, bestselling editions of Rumi's work! It's what we call "The Soup of the Soup of the Soup".'

In the years since my father's death, Occidental society has been flooded with all things Rumi.

Couplets ascribed to him are read solemnly at weddings across the United States, Europe, and beyond.

Wisdom drawn from his poetry is tattooed daily over the backs and limbs of Hollywood A-listers.

But the precious words uttered at weddings, tattooed into skin, and quoted in abundance, hold little or no bearing to the original verses of Jalaluddin Rumi.

So, there it is…

The great Sufi Master's wisdom available:

(a) in a form that's unreadable because it's all covered in glutinous gravy, or

(b) in another form that's completely distorted – the Soup of the Soup of the Soup.

One thing that *is* evident is that the West can benefit enormously from a clean, clear rendition of Rumi's thinking – as the East has done over the last seven hundred years.

For this reason, we have commissioned entirely new translations, gleaned in particular from *The Masnavi*. Selected and translated by native Persian-speaking scholars, the emphasis has been on maintaining the lightness of Rumi's poetry.

In an age of relentless speed and digital overload, and so as to allow the work to be accessed by those who may benefit from it most, we have arranged a series of bite-sized morsels by way of theme.

We encourage you to do what students, scholars, and ordinary people have done across the East for centuries...

To pick a single couplet, or a handful – and to read them over and over, allowing them to seed themselves in your mind.

Little by little, having taken root, they will blossom and bear fruit.

Tahir Shah

How to Use This Book

Rumi Readings for College

This book is for students – but not only in the academic sense.

It is for those navigating a time of change, challenge, and possibility.

For those exploring knowledge, identity, friendship, independence, meaning – sometimes all at once.

It is for the mind that's hungry, and the heart that's tired.

For the soul that wants to make sense of it all – or simply find stillness inside it.

College is a place of learning, yes.

But it's also a place of unlearning.

Of breaking. Of becoming.

Of wondering who you are when the lecture ends, the room empties, and you're left with your own thoughts.

Rumi Readings for College offers a still voice in the midst of all that motion.

These quotes, freshly translated from the original Persian, have been selected from Rumi's vast body of work – especially *The Masnavi*, known for its deep, transformative wisdom.

They are arranged in ten themed parts, touching on topics like knowledge, thought, questioning, teachers, self-reflection, and emotional development – all central to the student journey, whether in a classroom or in life.

There are no tests here. No grades.
Just the invitation to sit with a few lines at a time, and see what rises in you.

You Don't Have to Read It All

You can. But you don't have to.

This book is designed for dipping into. Skimming. Returning. Re-reading. You might read one quote a day. Or one a week. You might read five in one sitting, then nothing for a month. That's all fine.

There is no wrong way to engage with Rumi – except to treat it like something you need to 'master'. These are not lessons to be conquered. They are moments to be met.

Some days a quote will speak directly to your situation.
Other days it may puzzle you.
Let both experiences be part of the learning.

Let the Quote Find You

If you don't know where to begin, don't overthink it.

Open the book randomly. Let your eyes land somewhere. Start there.

What you find may feel like an accident – or it may feel like a message sent specifically to you. Either way, trust it. Rumi believed the soul knows where it's going, even when we don't.

Ask Your Own Questions

College teaches you to seek answers – in books, in classes, in data.
But Rumi teaches you to stay with your **questions** – not to rush them.

After reading a quote, ask yourself:

- What is this stirring in me?
- What part of me feels challenged, comforted, or curious?
- What if this quote is a doorway?

Write your response. Or simply think about it as you walk to class, make tea, or lie in bed. Ask more questions. Let them prompt memories. Or just write what you're feeling, even if it has nothing to do with the quote.

Read It When You're Struggling

You might not always feel focused. Or motivated. Or okay.

This book is for those times too.

Let it sit quietly on your shelf or in your bag – not demanding, just waiting.

When the stress builds, when you feel stuck or lost, open it. Read one line. Breathe.

Rumi's wisdom is not distant or abstract. It is grounded. Honest. Human.

He knew what it meant to feel overwhelmed, confused, or full of doubt.

He also knew that all of that could be the start of something extraordinary.

Share It – If You Want

These quotes were born in community. They've been shared aloud for centuries – in circles of students and seekers alike.

You may want to read one aloud in a study group.
Text one to a friend who's having a rough week.
Write one on a sticky note on your dorm door.

Sometimes, just one well-placed line can shift the whole energy of a space.

You never know what someone else is carrying.
Let the words be your offering.

Who You're Becoming

You're not just studying a subject.

You're studying **yourself** – in the truest, deepest sense. You're becoming someone. And that process is sacred.

Let this book be your mirror, your pause, your breath.

Let it remind you that achievement means nothing if you lose yourself – and that you already hold more wisdom than you know.

As Rumi writes:

'Strive to dispel the reservoir of ignorance from within yourself, allowing the morning to emerge brilliantly from the eastern depths of your soul.'

That morning is coming.

Keep reading. Keep asking. Keep showing up.

Part 1
The Meaning of Knowledge

1

Knowledge is the key to Solomon's kingdom;
it is the soul and essence of the world.
As the Creators of the plains, mountains and seas,
humanity would be powerless without this ability.

2

What is life?
It is recognizing right from wrong,
celebrating compassion,
and mourning when bad things happen.
Being aware of things is the essence of life;
so become more aware
if you want to be more alive.

3

Knowledge is the source
both of questions and answers,
just as soil and water
are the source of both thorns and flowers.

4

The wise person is the essence of law and piety,
and knowledge comes from their earlier austerity.
Knowledge is the sprouting seed,
and asceticism is the work put into the sowing.

5

A wealth of knowledge
can be misleading
when it turns into conceit
and leads you astray.

6

Many scholars are deprived of true knowledge:
they possess information,
but do not embody it.

7

When you see a mirage in the distance,
you instinctively rush towards it,
only to realize that you are captivated
by your own illusion.

8

You are not defined
by your physical body;
you are the essence of perception.
By perceiving the soul,
you can transcend the limitations of the body
and achieve freedom.
The essence of a person lies in their vision,
while the physical body is merely a vessel.
A person's true nature is shaped
by what their eyes have witnessed.

9

Those who find the path to enlightenment
through solitude
do not rely on external sources or knowledge.
Their vision transcends ordinary knowledge,
surpassing the mundane world.

10

Every response received by the heart
through the sense of hearing
is evaluated by the eye which says,
'Heed my guidance and ignore the rest.'
The ear acts as a conduit for communication,
while the eye fosters a deeper connection.
The eye holds wisdom and insight,
whereas the ear is linked to verbal expression.

Part 2

Routes to Obtaining Knowledge

11

The distinction between an explorer and an imitator
is profound.
The explorer can be likened to David,
a figure of original insight and action,
while the imitator is merely a reflection,
lacking depth and innovation.

12

Imitative knowledge is a cumbersome weight on our soul:
it is acquired from others,
yet we mistakenly attribute it to ourselves.
This lifeless knowledge appeals only to those
who seek superficially,
without true engagement.

13

Imitative knowledge can be bought and sold,
becoming highly visible once a transaction is made.
By contrast, investigative knowledge is pursued
for its own sake,
albeit with an always-thriving market for its wares.

14

Understanding deep emotion is a valuable skill,
while a grasping after superficial matters is a heavy burden.
Profound knowledge
that resonates deeply within you
becomes a cherished asset,
while superficial knowledge
that only scratches the surface,
can be a hindrance.

15

Knowledge has dual faculties,
while doubt possesses only one.
Due to this inherent limitation,
doubt's ability to soar is restricted.
The bird of uncertainty flutters unsteadily,
with only one wing,
and struggles to find a stable nest.
When uncertainty is removed,
genuine understanding emerges,
granting the bird its second wing
and allowing it to ascend.

16

Be aware that negative ideas
act like poisonous thorns
penetrating the depths of the soul,
and lead only to rumination.
The struggle to untangle complexities
wastes precious time and effort.

17

Existence revolves around principles and topics
that lack true discernment,
often driven by superficial or contrived efforts.
Any argument that fails to produce meaningful results
or proves ineffectual is rendered null and void.
It is crucial to critically examine the outcomes
of such arguments.

18

Imitative knowledge is purely pedagogical,
often evoking sorrow in its listeners.
Those who genuinely seek knowledge
aim to benefit both society and themselves,
and they strive to stay connected
with the realities of the world.

19

Knowledge that lacks direct engagement
is inherently precarious,
like the glimpse of a fleeting colour.

20

They purified their hearts with these discoveries,
for this wisdom is unaware of that path.
Knowledge must originate from a reliable source,
as every branch of knowledge is linked to its origin.

Part 3

Obstacles to Acquiring Knowledge

21

Despite having the ability to perceive,
individuals are often blinded and deafened
by their own greed and avarice.
While physical blindness can draw compassion,
the blindness caused by greed
is persistent and unyielding.

22

Lust distorts and impairs the heart's perceptive capacity,
turning a donkey into 'Joseph', and fire into 'light'.
This deception must be recognized
as a false perception along the way.

23

Those who, driven by envy,
take out another's eye,
ultimately deprive themselves
of their own ears and nose.

24

Every sceptic asserts
that they will not heed the truth,
even if it is confirmed by numerous signs.
When confronted with evidence,
those whose minds are dominated by imagination
tend to further entrench their fantastical beliefs.

25

I observed the house with its many adornments,
and was disturbed by my intense desire to own it.
The wise man remarked,
'You are like a child surrounded
by an abundance of decorations.'

26

Given that imitation is intrinsically connected
to the core of your being,
it is essential to cleanse its hold on you with tears.
Imitation is a destructive force
that undermines all virtue,
no matter how formidable it may seem,
even if it were as towering as a mountain.

27

Existence can induce a state of intoxication,
blurring the intellect and removing inhibitions
from the emotions.
For thousands of years, the allure of life has led many
astray from their true path.

28

Fortunate is the person
who acknowledges their own shortcomings,
for those who criticize faults in others
often find those very flaws reflected back on themselves.
Half of these issues stem from their own errors,
while the other half arise from what is imperceptible.
If you have ten wounds on your head,
you must tend to them yourself.

29

Avoid drawing parallels
between your own behaviour
and that of the morally just,
even if words like 'lion' and 'milk'[1]
may seem similar when written down.
The entire world has strayed from the right path
due to such misunderstandings,
and only a few individuals
truly grasp the essence of virtue.

---

1   Both 'lion' and 'milk' are written شیر in Persian.

30

Rage warps and distorts an individual's resolve,
transforming steadfast strength of character into chaos.
Anger clouds artistic expression,
creating numerous barriers between the heart and the eyes.

Part 4

The Role of Knowledge in Human Relationships

31

Guiding those who remain unaware
due to their own ignorance
is like planting seeds in infertile soil.
The irreparable damage caused by folly and ignorance
often renders such efforts futile.
It is generally unwise to invest valuable knowledge
in those who are unwilling or unable to appreciate it.

32

Associating with fools
can be detrimental,
as it detracts from the pursuit of enlightenment
that, ideally, you should seek.

33

Hearts bound by illusion
will only see their delusions reinforced,
even when presented with rational explanations.
Engaging in conversation with such people
can be counterproductive,
much like a warrior's sword in the hands of a thief.

34

A bird that sings off-key
should be silenced,
just as the excuses of a fool
should be disregarded.
An apology from such a person
can often be more harmful
than their original mistake.
Similarly, the excuses of the ignorant act
as a toxic force,
undermining and destroying knowledge.

35

If someone is not worthy of these words and prayers,
then the appropriate response to a fool,
Your Majesty, is silence.
The heavens themselves respond in silence,
as if acknowledging this wisdom.

36

He gave the instruction:
Avoid the fool!
Leave, and free yourself.
Do not hold me back!

37

A leader lacking mental strength is deeply confused,
unable to see what lies behind or ahead
due to their own foolishness.
The path may appear clear,
but hidden dangers lie beneath,
and the abundance of superficial labels
masks a lack of true significance.

38

Disarm the deranged,
ensuring that justice and righteousness
find contentment in your actions.
He possesses power without wisdom,
so it is crucial to restrain him
to prevent widespread harm.

39

Unworthy people
who possess wealth and power
inevitably bring shame upon themselves.
They may exhibit parsimony,
leading to diminished charitable contributions,
or display excessive generosity
inappropriate in its application.

40

If a traitor wields the pen,
it is certain that the virtuous
will ultimately face execution on the gallows.

Part 5

The Role of Questioning in Acquiring Knowledge

41

Half of your knowledge is gained
through asking questions,
yet not everyone has the opportunity to do so.

42

You ask why an action is taken.
The form is visible, like oil,
while its essence is 'light'.
But why ask a question that has no purpose?
The form is crafted to express the essence.
Enquiry is meaningful
only if it serves a purpose;
otherwise, it is futile.

43

When a thorn pierces someone's foot,
they lift it and inspect the wound,
using a needle if necessary.
If they can't find the thorn,
they show discomfort or pain.
Locating a thorn in the foot is challenging.
But imagine the difficulty
of addressing a thorn embedded in the heart.
If people could perceive the thorns
within their own hearts,
all grief would cease.

44

We possess a deep enthusiasm
for engaging in complex debates,
and relish unravelling intricate problems.
Our aim is to untangle and understand complexities,
enhancing our comprehension
through the exchange of questions and answers.

45

Although you may see the outward form,
you may not grasp its deeper significance.
If you possess wisdom,
choose a pearl from the shell.
However, remember that not every shell contains a gem.
To uncover these hidden treasures,
you must carefully observe
and delve into the depths of each person's essence.

46

The leader does not ease my burden,
nor does he grant me access
to the depths of my innermost thoughts.
His intense gaze burns like a flame,
and his probing questions,
sweet as nectar,
have captured my fascination.

47

He extended his hand
and took a seat beside him,
as love embraced his heart and soul.
The other, in a gesture of respect,
kissed his hands and forehead
while expressing curiosity
about his well-being and direction in life.
He persistently posed questions
until he attained a position of great honour, proclaiming,
'Through patience and enquiry
I have discovered a priceless treasure.'

48

Avoid enquiries
into the reasons behind someone's curiosity
regarding the phases of the moon,
or seeking specifics about its terminology,
temporal patterns,
or hierarchical classification.

49

A person who questioned the purpose
was met with silence,
followed by profound sorrow.
Reflecting on this, they wondered,
'Why did I seek this information?'
And were left with feelings of sadness and regret.

50

People with a gentle nature
and a talent for healing emotional wounds
are often impelled to enquire
about the well-being of others,
especially those caught in struggle.

Part 6

The Role of Thought in Acquiring Knowledge

51

Consider the mind and esteemed spirit
as the true essence of a person,
for it is through thought
that one gains value and significance.

52

In the beginning the world was created through thought followed by action.

53

Flies congregate on a wound,
oblivious to their own repugnance.
The flies symbolize your thoughts, and money,
while your wound represents the gloom
of your current state.

54

Ensure that your thoughts are not distorted,
but rather focused and accurate;
for thoughts are the illuminating essence
of a precious gem.

.

55

Each cognitive process engulfs and absorbs another;
one thought consumes and assimilates the next.

56

Exert less effort in unravelling knots,
for your wings and feathers
may gradually be damaged
by the intensity and force of it.
Despite fracturing their wings,
many birds persevered
through dangers without turning back.

57

Any reasoning not derived from divine revelation
is driven by personal desire.
Such thoughts are like dust in the air,
disparate, and lacking substance.

58

Witness the boundless manifestations
stemming from a solitary idea,
cascading ceaselessly across the surface of the planet.
Though this idea may appear insignificant to some,
it possesses the power to engulf
and profoundly alter the world,
like a flood.

59

Our thinking is a projectile launched
from the divine realm into the atmosphere.
How can it sustain its position in the air?
In the end, it is surrendered back to the divine.

60

Thinking and reflection
are like a narrow channel,
, while revelation and discovery
resemble the vast expanse of the sky and clouds.

Part 7

The Role of a Mentor
in Gaining Knowledge

61

God is the sole entity possessing knowledge
that is self-contained and unaffected
by external factors.
Just as God imparted knowledge directly to Adam
without intermediaries or barriers,
humans must also make serious efforts
to extract fundamental truths
from the complexities of life.

62

Swiftly and confidently seize the edge of their garment
to find a path in the final era.
When navigating this challenging terrain,
it is crucial to have this guide by your side.
Express your reluctance to part ways
with those who are leaving,
as Khalil[2] did.

---

2   Another name for the Prophet Abraham.

63

Among the fakirs,
assess them carefully,
and choose the one
who is truly genuine.

64

Select a seasoned individual as your mentor,
for lacking such guidance
will lead to a journey fraught
with hardships, anxiety, and peril.
Venturing alone on an unfamiliar path is unwise.
It is prudent to have a guide,
and to stay close to someone who knows.

65

Only place your trust
in the hand of someone seasoned,
as their guidance is rooted in Truth.
By clasping your hand with theirs,
you will find protection
from those who seek to mislead you.

66

Expect a mentor
to rescue you,
and guide you out of danger.

67

Those who embark on the path without a guide
may turn a two-day trip
into a journey of a hundred years.
Anyone who rushes to the Kaaba
without proper guidance
will become disoriented and embarrassed,
and wander aimlessly.

68

The person of discernment
found delight in his words,
yet also experienced bitterness
in his company.
His external aspect indicated agility,
yet his impact weakened the spirit.

69

Those who travel this path infrequently on their own
will receive valuable assistance and knowledge
from the wise.

70

The elderly gentleman of summer
and the youngsters of July
contrast sharply.
The youth may embody the darkness of the night,
while the elderly person shines
with the luminosity of the moon.

Part 8

What Makes
a Genuine Student?

71

When the learned man observed
the servant of small stature,
he signalled for another person to approach.
My reference to the letter of mercy
was not meant to undermine its importance.
Similarly, when a father affectionately calls his child,
'My little one,'
it is not intended to belittle
or show disrespect.

72

When the listener has thirst and enthusiasm,
even if the preacher were devoid of life,
they would become animated and able to communicate.

73

Upon the arrival of an attentive and unburdened listener,
even those who are unable to speak
are endowed with a multitude of voices.

74

Just as a child placed in a tailor's shop
must comply with the master
if he is given the task of weaving a mat:
he should start weaving it;
and if asked to sew,
then he should sew.
If someone desires to acquire tailoring skills,
whether through manual stitching,
or the use of a needle,
they must relinquish personal judgement
and submit to the authority of the master.

75

Strive to dispel the reservoir of ignorance
from within yourself,
allowing the morning to emerge brilliantly
from the eastern depths of your soul.

76

A friend serves as a reflection of the soul
during times of sadness.
Would you intentionally blur a mirror
by breathing on it?
To prevent it from concealing itself,
you must control each and every one of your breaths.

77

Without rainfall,
how can the garden thrive?
Without the child crying,
the milk cannot flow.
Even an infant has the innate wisdom
to cry in a way
that elicits the presence of the caring nurse.

78

Solutions tend to gravitate
toward challenging questions,
just as water naturally fills the spaces
around a ship at sea.
Instead of actively searching for water,
cultivate a sense of thirst within yourself,
allowing water to flow naturally
from both above and below.

79

As the audience dozed off,
the river swiftly swept away the millstones.
Since you no longer need the mill,
redirect the water to its primary course.
We use the term 'mill' as a metaphor
representing a source of guidance and instruction.

80

The effect of spring rainfall on a tree
depends on the tree's own inherent vitality.
If a tree remains barren despite the nourishing breeze,
the fault lies not with the breeze,
but with the tree itself.

Part 9
What Makes a Teacher?

81

The gardener, favoured by destiny,
cannot distinguish between trees,
nor can they determine
which tree bears bitter fruit
and which yields fruit
equal to seven hundred others.
How can they cultivate them equally
when viewed through the lens of accumulated
knowledge and skills?

82

Communicate with the bird of destiny
using the language of inevitability.
Address the bird with broken wings
in the dialect of forbearance.
Value the resilient bird and show forgiveness,
and describe the legendary creature
endowed with the attributes of the phoenix.

83

Mustafa[3] himself stated that every prophet
regardless of age
fulfilled the role of a shepherd.
Those who refuse to undertake this trial
have not been bestowed
with leadership by Truth.

---

3   Another name for the Prophet Muhammad.

84

Despite being struck a hundred times,
I shall continue to radiate light,
like a candle.
If the fire engulfs
both before and after,
the moon will still be enough for the night.

85

Communicate in a manner
that enhances the general understanding
and knowledge of the audience.
An ideal speaker can be likened
to a lavish banquet,
with a diverse array of culinary delights.
The banquet he hosts
provides nourishment for every guest,
each individual finding sustenance to suit their taste.

86

Acquiring knowledge necessitates
the reception of information
through spoken communication.
Acquiring skills requires
the practical demonstration of that knowledge.

87

When Mustafa found great pleasure in the story,
his desire to continue speaking grew even stronger.
When Mustafa, the listener,
becomes fully engaged,
every hair on his body turns into a speaking tongue.

88

A fatigued and debilitated sheep fell behind.
Moses, the divinely chosen one,
brushed the dust off it.
He tenderly caressed its back and head,
offering comfort and attention,
just like a mother.

89

Though the teacher,
like a donkey,
shared confidential information with the fox,
he spoke carelessly,
mimicking without true understanding.
He expressed admiration for water,
yet lacked a sincere desire for it.
He tore his garments,
but did not exhibit the fervour of a true admirer.

90

When you place your hand
in the hand of a wise elder,
the elder endowed with wisdom,
who possesses profound knowledge and meaning.

Part 10

The Practice
of Appreciation

91

As the holder of the pen,
you have the power
to shape the world like a canvas.
Your words have the ability
to create and refine.

92

Emulate our state of being,
that brims with elation;
in the garden,
be like the upright cypress tree.
When you are in the presence of people
who embody love,
my discerning friend,
allow your heart to be receptive,
like a compassionate teacher.

93

Any heart that finds joy in your absence
is as insignificant and fleeting
as chaff carried by the wind.
Just as a tamed bird yearns to fly freely,
a scholar without the guidance of an instructor
remains directionless.

94

What is the reason
behind the profound wisdom
and mastery of your love?
What is the reason
behind the delicate foundation
of your affection?

95

I was drunk
and asked my teacher to give me
clear understanding
of existence and non-existence.
He replied,
telling me to leave,
and that by distancing myself
from the tribulations of others,
I would discover peace.

96

Master,
you are easily influenced
by every passing thought,
swiftly transitioning
from sadness to happiness in a moment.
Observing your presence amidst the flames,
I chose not to intervene,
allowing you the opportunity
to undergo a process of refinement,
acquire wisdom, and develop mastery.

97

Despite the capture of my teacher's bird
by the master's trap,
I wholeheartedly dedicated myself to them,
experiencing a state of euphoria
and carefree joy in their service.

98

All things,
whether the moon or a fish,
offer praise with modesty,
but the teacher's wisdom
reveals it with greater clarity.
The stones shed tears,
and the heavens bestow blessings
when the teacher imparts lessons
of profound understanding.

99

While I stopped trying,
my heart remained restless;
though everyone else gave up,
their spirit never found a moment of rest.
Those who commit themselves
to mastering a particular skill
will ultimately succeed.
But the highest level of mastery
is attained by those who strive
for improvement without cease.

100

He has captivated the entire world,
as if their physical beings have merged
with their spiritual essence.
To evaluate them,
he has altered their external appearances
through the affection of the expert.

Finis

www.ingramcontent.com/pod-product-compliance
Lightning Source LLC
Chambersburg PA
CBHW020450100426
42813CB00031B/3314/J